Strategy

Understanding, Formulating & Implementing Strategies for Success

Table of Contents

Introduction   3

Chapter 1: What Is A Strategy?   5

Chapter 2: Understanding Different Types Of Strategies   9

Chapter 3: Why A Business Should Have A Strategy   14

Chapter 4: Mastering The Art Of Strategy Formulation   20

Chapter 5: Becoming A Master-The 3Cs Of Strategy Implementation   24

Chapter 6: The Ins And Outs of Reviewing a Strategy- Tips on How to Run a successful Strategy Review Meeting   28

Conclusion   31

Introduction

If there is one thing I have learnt over many years of learning from my mistakes, it has to be the importance of a strategy in everything I do.

As I have realized, the need for a strategy is something most of us fail to do or account for as we plan our lives and businesses. This is regardless of the fact that without a detailed strategy on how to implement whatever progress or project, it will fail regardless of how well detailed the habit, plan, or business is.

Let me ask you question. How many times have you failed to plan and strategize on something of importance only to have it fail? My guess would be many times.

Let us be bluntly honest for a minute. When we talk about formulating a strategy, to most of people, a business related strategy pops into the mind. Did you know that making even the smallest positive change in your life demands the use of a strategy?

Let us look at an example. If you want to change something in your life, say for example you want to lose weight, hitting the gym like a maniac without a detailed plan of attack such as which muscles to exercise during a daily workout routine, or how to eat healthy as you exercise, will yield minimal results.

Creating or formulating a strategy is one of those skills that each one of us should learn. Fortunately, formulating a strategy is not as hard as you may have been led to believe.

This book will show you just how easy it is to formulate a strategy and use that strategy to implement infinite positive change in your business or life.

Chapter 1: What Is A Strategy?

There are many understandings and definitions of the word strategy. Unfortunately, this is not a good thing because it means that in some cases, the true meaning of the word strategy erodes as many people use different meanings to define it.

Nevertheless, the word strategy is derived from the Greek word stratēgia, which means the art of troop leader or office of general command general ship. Whenever we use Greek to explain anything, the explanation tends to be long and complicated. This is not the case with strategy.

If we were to break it down completely, a strategy is a detailed plan of action on how to achieve one or more life or business goals regardless of the conditions or uncertainty. The use of the term strategy stems from the early 6th century CE in East Roman empire. As a word, strategy was not translated into Western vernacular until the 20th century.

In our day-to-day activities and living, having a strategy is important because in general, resources available to help you reach your goals are generally limited. A strategy involves detailed actions geared towards specific goals achievement, goals setting, and organising resources to achieve your success.

A strategy can also be a planned pattern of doing things or activities as an individual or a business to adapt to the environment and challenges in it. When you have a strategy before starting anything, it is easier to achieve goals taking into account the available resources.

In finding solutions to problems or achieving goals for the future, there must be a plan and a detailed process. In this case, there is need to carefully analyse what you currently have, predicting changes in the market and planning on future success and achievements. Let me emphasize that it is always important to plan for success. This is because planning helps you know and implement all the advantages and opportunities open to you. This way, you'll be fully prepared on how to pursue the future depending on your goals and achievements.

Productive organizations create strategies to guide them into the future. This helps and enables those leading it to determine how the business develops and competes with other businesses in the future.

A strategy is also a method you plan to use to determine what you will achieve in the future. It defines how you will achieve whatever goals you set forth be it for business or personal. Often times, it may refer to the long-term scope and direction of your life or business. This enables an individual, a company, or an organisation to achieve and meet the market needs, deal with environmental challenges and use the necessary resources to achieve set goals. This allows one to know what a business needs for better performance, the businesses ability to compete and factors to consider that may have an effect on external, internal and environmental factors related to the business or overall development. Strategy also helps you know about the values and expectations of the business as well as the stakeholders.

Earlier on, we mentioned something about a strategy meaning different things to different people. The reason for this is mainly because there are different types of strategies all geared towards specific areas of one's life or business. In the next chapter, we shall delve into understanding different types of strategies.

Chapter 2: Understanding Different Types of Strategies

If we are being honest, even if you know nothing about strategies, their use or effectiveness, it is highly likely that at one point or the other, you have unknowingly used a strategy. For example, to pass your exams, you must have done a lot of studying. Did you just wing it or did you create a timeline of when, what and how to study? To most people, the latter holds true.

As indicated, a strategy is a detailed plan of action. In our example, the plan would be what time to study, what subject or topic to study on a specific day, and the amount of time dedicated to studying. As indicated earlier, strategies cut across individual persona and transcends into organizations. In fact, in any particular organisation or in your life, strategies exist at several different levels.

Often times, these strategies differ from person to person, organization to organization, and business to business. What does this mean? It means that in formulating a strategy for your business or personal growth, you must first have a clear understanding of various strategies. The following is a list of the different types of strategies.

#1 Contraction Strategy

This strategy deals with the general purpose of a business geared towards meeting stakeholders' expectations. It is an important strategy because it draws most of its influence from business investors.

A contract strategy acts as a guide through which the business makes decisions. The strategy's main purpose is to focus on the products that bring more profits and do away with low-profit goods or services.

A contraction strategy may include divestiture where an already operating unit is sold if and when a business decides to completely and permanently leave a market despite the current market's capability. This may happen due to the business need to concentrate on other long-term growth operations.

#2 Business Unit Strategies

A business unit strategy may refer to a planned guide and objective mainly set by the business management to be followed as a guide through sovereign participation of an organisation. This allows for preparation and is used in large businesses to have different considerable objectives among different work divisions.

Mainly in a particular market, for a business or an organisation to successfully compete, a business unit strategy comes in handy because it has everything to do with production choices, meeting customer needs, attaining and achieving more than the competitor, and creating and exploiting new opportunities.

#3 Operational Strategies

Most businesses and organisations have different segments with different roles and measures working together or put in place to provide the direction that the business-unit level must take to become profitable.

An operational strategy mainly focuses and deals with allocation of resources, procedures and other factors that influence the optimum operation of the business unit. An operational strategy provides direction to serve the agenda of the business and carry out specific functions of the organisation. It acts as a structural guide and helps in analysis of growth capabilities to enable the company compete at a level playing field.

#4 Teamwork Strategies

For a business or organization to succeed, all facets, departments and individuals must work together as a team. A teamwork strategy outlines how different teams and departments will work together for the business unit success. For example, while one team works towards the achievement of set goals by providing a specific but different contribution, another team, no matter how small the team is, may work on a different facet of the same goal another team may be working towards. This can make achieving goals geared towards business success easier.

Teamwork strategy is an essential part of any business because it works as a support beam for different departments working towards the success of a business. One important consideration to have in mind when formulating a business strategy is considering how best to implement best practices aimed at facilitating the teams as they work towards meeting each team's objective.

Now that we have looked at the meaning of strategy and the different types of strategies, it is important that we understand why a strategy is very important. We will look at this in the next chapter.

Chapter 3: Why a Business Should Have a Strategy

In order for your business to flourish and meet set goals, you need multiple, well-defined strategies. Part of the reason for this is that without a strategy, your business or organisation will fail. Thus, a strategy is not only a significantly vital part of your business success; it is also a vital part of any personal development or achievement.

Although there are many personal and business benefits to creating a strategy, let us look at some of the more important ones.

#1 Increased Familiarity

To have a clear understanding of your business tenet and drive it towards success, a strategy comes in very handy.

A strategy helps you understand a business' central capabilities. It helps you identify weak links in your business and find solutions to the problem thus reducing the business risk factors. This enables the business to have a better view of what they need to do or progress towards to increase performance, production and essentially, profits. Moreover, a strategy, be it any of the ones we touched on earlier will help you understand or give you a glimpse of how the business is performing financially, allow you proper insight into workforce turnover, customer satisfaction, etc.

Familiarity with your business will enable you to list the business weaknesses, strengths, threats and the opportunities, which may be associated with your business.

Moreover, different strategies help you know and understand a lot about your business external environment and market competition. This can give you a well-deserved advantage over your competitors

#2: Supports Growth

It is always important to understand and acknowledge changes in your business environment and market. By creating a strategy, you steer your business in the right direction factoring in the market and competition needs. This will ensure the long-term profitability of your business.

Normally, businesses experience change day in day out. Even though the changes may be slight, they can often have adverse effects on a business or organization. For your business to adapt to these changes and limit their potential effect, you must know how to respond to social, political or technology driven adjustments.

A strategy, for example a focus strategy, can help you strategize on how to drive long-term growth, how to tap growth opportunities and sustain business profitability. Moreover, when you recognize your business shortcomings, you can help the business adapt to changing business dynamics that may have a negative impact on the business bottom line.

#3: Helps in identifying and achieving objectives

For a business to move from one level to another, be it in terms of production, profitability, or otherwise, there is need for a working strategy. This is especially important in identifying the key steps you need to chart your business towards as you drive it towards the achievement of set goals and standards.

You may be wondering how a strategy may help you identify your business objectives. How is easy. When you create a strategy, regardless of the type of strategy, you create a path that your business will follow. The path you create stems from the direction you want the business to head towards.

Once you define objectives and create a path towards their achievement, you can keep abreast with all information and requirements enabling you to push beyond those achievements and chart more goals. By identifying the framework you need to use or the road to follow towards your targets and business achievement, implementing is needed to get better results.

#4: Helps in communication and dedication

When you have a strategic plan for your business and company, transparency and individual accountability is illuminated. This way, you can create a well-organised and accomplished organization that drives forth team communication. This encourages dedication for every individual at any level of the business. Essentially, a strategy helps you understand and pinpoint, compare and contrast individual or team performance and accountability.

#5: Creates vision and direction

Generally, a business without a strategy has no direction. If your business operates without a strategy, it is highly likely that staff within the organization or business will operate from a place of no vision or direction where nothing takes priority.

A strategy provides a business or organisation with a general purpose in terms of goals and their achievement. Further, it defines roles. This ensures allocation of individuals and resources to meet set goals and objectives.

Other than the five reasons above, strategies also help in creation of new business opportunities, reorganising the operations of the business and staff engagement. This allows the business or organization in development and growth. This can spearhead development and business profitability in the long term.

Now that you know how important strategy is for the growth and success of a business, we will now look at how to formulate strategy.

Chapter 4: Mastering the Art of Strategy Formulation

For a business or organisation to accomplish its goals and attain symbiosis in terms of profitability and operation, there must be a plan that carries the business forward from where it is to where it ought to be. Doing this i.e. formulating a strategy helps the business continuously reach its goals as well as enabling the business adopt different strategies driven by changing business and market dynamics.

Strategy formulation involves a sequence of steps performed and adapted continuously. Unfortunately, there is a huge misconception that formulating a strategy is a backbreaking task. There is some truth to this notion. However, it does not understate the importance of a strategy. In fact, a strategy is so important that without it, it is hard to accomplish anything regardless of what it is. Although developing and formulating a strategy may seem like a huge task, it is easier than you may have thought. Let us look at the steps needed to create a strategic plan that works.

Step #1: Start by determining where you are

The first step to creating a vibrant strategic plan is by determining where you are. While this may seem easy, it is actually a bit difficult than it seems. The reason for the difficulty is that most business and individuals see themselves and their businesses as how they want rather than how it is or how it appears to others. This is a fatal mistake and one that you must avoid at all cost. Why?

This is simply because an accurate picture of where your business is will allow you to conduct internal and external audits of your business and its market dynamics. The trick to this is to determine your business's real competencies and not perceived ones.

Step #2: Ascertain what's important

After determining where you are, the next step is focusing on the direction you want to take over a specific period. This is very useful in that it helps set the direction the enterprise will pursue over time and clearly defines the mission and vision.

From this analysis, it is then easier to determine what should take first priority. For example, if a certain issue holds more collateral in terms of its overall effect on the business, you can give it the proper attention it deserves before it affects the business.

Step #3: Define intended achievements

Define all expected objectives and using step two above, succinctly state all your intended achievements and what your business or organization must do to achieve these goals and achievements in relation to their priority.

Step #4: Define and determine level of accountability

The only way to take your business or organization to where you want it to be is by determining accountability. In this respect, strategies, action plans, budget and manpower resources you need are all essential steps you need to take to determine how you will allocate all resources including human and monetary capital and how or who will be responsible with handling and dealing with priority issues in relation to objective and goal accomplishment.

Step #5: Review, tweak, review…re-tweak

The truth is that the process of formulating a strategy is a never-ending one. After formulating a plan, to ensure that it performs as defined, there is need to do a detailed analysis of the implementation process. After reviewing, you must tweak what works, eliminate what doesn't work and add other facets that you think may work better.

You cannot make any progress in life if you simply set strategies but fail to implement them. Up to this moment, we have outlined the importance of a strategic plan, looked at the different types of strategies, and looked at how to formulate a strategy. In the next bit, we shall look at implementing a strategy.

Chapter 5: Becoming a Master- The 3Cs of Strategy Implementation

As we have seen, a strategy is an important part of any achievement especially in business. It allows a company or organization to focus on the important areas that can drive it towards defined achievements. Unfortunately, most business leaders or organization heads allocate a lot of time to strategy formulation and very little time or effort into implementing the set strategy.

The successful implementation of a strategy demands the concerted effort and attention of everyone in the organization or company. However, often, it is the work or leaders to create, monitor and determine what demands focus at any given time and in a way that allows each aspect of the strategy to come alive throughout the organization.

In this respect, and in implementing a strategy, it is always wise to pay attention to the 3Cs of strategy.

Clarify

A strategy is often times an expressed high-level statement that echoes well in the boardroom with the executives and board members but falls short or reverberating with the mid-level and frontline company staff.

This is very sad because if employees within a company or organization do not comprehend and understand a strategy, there will be a marginal disconnect between formulating a strategy and implementing it. Therefore, the first step in implementing a strategy is making sure that the strategy and its tenets are clear to the people that will implement it. This way, it is easier for people in your organization to rally behind the strategy and concentrate on its implementation.

If you do this part well, your strategy will tie in with your objectives and goals and clearly define what you intend to do and how you intend to do it.

Communicate

In an organization, there is nothing like too much communication. Communication is the second C in strategy implementation. As you work towards the implementation of your strategy, you have to powerfully communicate the essence of your strategy at even the lowest level of your organization.

Fortunately, you can communicate the essence of the strategy in many different ways. For example, you can use the company's message board, internal blog or even posters.

Discussions at every possible moment are also a very effective way of articulating and translating the meat of your strategy to company staff. Communicating the strategy in an easy to understand way creates the bridge needed to take the strategy paper from being just another paper to actionable information.

Cascade

A strategy defines what you want to do and how you intend to do it. If the implementation of a strategy is to be successful, there is need to cascade the strategy throughout the organization. This is essential in that it nails down the tactical and practical mechanisms of each person's job on a daily basis.

Doing this is a crucial step because it allows managers within the organization the 'power' they need to take charge of the strategy and its implementation within specific departments. Cascading your strategy is the stock of strategy implementation and is where most of the bulk work goes. In this respect, cascading may include team meetings, process improvements, responses to the market and other external factors, one-on-one coaching and everything else that aligns with the meat of the strategy.

Learning how to effectively implement a strategy is a very important part especially considering that most businesses are often engaged in stiff competition for a share of the market. Therefore, successfully implementing a strategy can give the business the competitive edge it needs to dominate a market and drive up profits.

Chapter 6: The Ins And Outs of Reviewing a Strategy- Tips on How to run a successful Strategy Review Meeting

As we have continuously indicated, strategic plans are not set in stone. In fact, your strategy should be fluid in order to allow tweaks to extenuating factors. Actually, effective organizations continuously revisit their strategic plan and view the plans as anchors and not as constraints to the achievement of the company's objectives.

Formulating a strategy and learning how to implement it successfully demands reviewing and re-tweaking as we stated earlier. As we also stated earlier, your strategy should be fluid to cater for changes influenced by changing dynamics be they from a business or personal perspective. As we have also continuously seen, a strategy is about making choices about where you or your organization wants to be and creating a plan on how to get there. This requires reviewing.

Unfortunately, most people within an organization involved with the implementation of a strategy find meetings to be a total bore and rightly so because too many company heads run meetings very poorly without any real objective and end up wasting the employees' time. To aid you in your strategy review process and equip you with the skills you need to make all your strategy meetings productive and focused, below are four effective tips.

#1: Make your Strategy the Agenda

Even though a strategy review meeting is a different kind of meeting, it is still a meeting nonetheless: a meeting based on your strategy. Therefore, it is only right that you should treat it as such, and have an agenda solely focused on your strategic plan. In the meeting, you should move to cover the most important bits of the agenda or strategic plan as quick as possible and acknowledge any progress you may have accomplished toward the attainment of your objective or goals. Making your strategy the main agenda will help you steer the meeting in the right direction and keep the meeting focused on the strategy rather than letting the meeting derail into other concerns.

#2: Outline topics early

Awesome meetings do not happen by magic: they are planned. To run a successful review meeting, you must plan. This means outlining agenda topics well in advance of the actual strategy meeting. If you gather all the information you need to chart the strategy meeting in the direction you want, you are ensuring that everything of importance receives its fair share of coverage during the meeting.

#3: Document all decisions

Keep a log of everything you discussed in previous meetings and the decisions that were made during those meetings. In the documents, succinctly document and outline who was accountable for specific actions and the timeline by which a specific action needed review.

#4: Monitor

Here is a question for you. How many times have you had the same meeting covering the same topic? My guess would be many times. If you monitor all your strategy meetings and their follow-ups, it is easier to monitor decisions made from meeting to meeting.

Conclusion

A strategy and the entire process of formulating one, implementing one and reviewing one is not a destination. Do not expect to formulate a strategy today and successfully implement it tomorrow. Successful implementation of a strategy is a journey. A journey that demands perseverance, patience and a lot of determination to tweak what works, discard what does not work, and re-implement until your strategic plan helps you achieve your goals be it personal or business related.

www.ingramcontent.com/pod-product-compliance
Lightning Source LLC
Chambersburg PA
CBHW070430190526
45169CB00003B/1493